A Rich Heritage

A Rich Heritage

Charles Greig

with photographs by
J. D. Rattar

The Shetland Times Ltd.,
Lerwick.
2003.

A Rich Heritage

Copyright © Charles Greig, 2003.

ISBN 1 898852 93 6

First published by The Shetland Times Ltd., 2003.

All rights reserved.
No part of this publication may be reproduced, stored in a retrieval system, or transmitted, in any form, or by any means, electronic, mechanical, photocopying, recording or otherwise, without the prior written permission of the publishers.

British Library Cataloguing-in-Publication Data
A catalogue record for this books is available from the British Library.

Published and printed by
The Shetland Times Ltd.,
Gremista, Lerwick
Shetland ZE1 0PX, UK

To my parents.

Acknowledgements

I wish to express my thanks to all who have inspired in me a love of Shetland and its traditions and have encouraged me to write these verses. J. D. Rattar's photographs continue to open views to a bygone age and remind us of our rich heritage. Copies of his work may be obtained from the Shetland Museum.

I am especially grateful to those who have allowed me to share their experiences and have permitted me to publish "their" poems. Mr John J. Graham has given me invaluable assistance and I am also indebted to others for their advice and support.

Shetland Verses

with traditional scenes

Contents

List of illustrations 11

Our Heritage

1. Mousa 13
2. Young Love 14
3. Erlend and Margaret 15
4. The Ruin at Westerwick 16
5. Mattie's Trip ta Lerrick 18
6. Journey to Wick 20
7. The Contentment of the Uneasy Chair 22

Birth and Childhood

8. Expectant Joy 25
9. Ailsa 26
10. A Baptismal Blessing 27
11. A Sunny Day with Rachel 28
12. Georgia 29
13. A Lovely Peerie Bairn 31
14. The School 32

The Middle Years

15. The Bride 33
16. The Wedding – at Cullivoe 34

Reflections

17. Ode to Dr Robertson 35
18. The Knitting 37
19. The Peat Hill 38
20. Lerwick after the Last Half-Century 39
21. Pictures on the Wall 42
22. The Storm 43

Those We Have Loved

23. Grant 44
24. Bryan 45
25. The Widow's Mites 46
26. Candice 47
27. Memories Shared 48
28. At The Ness Kirk 49
29. Kathleen 50
30. Gathered Grief 52
31. A Quiet and Gentle Life 53
32. Maggie Ann 54
33. Those we have loved 55

Illustrations

The Haven under the Hill – *J. D. Rattar*	7
A Lerwick Lane – *J. D. Rattar*	8
Crofts, Vidlin – *J. D. Rattar*	10
Pictish Tower, Mousa – *J. D. Rattar*	15
Woman with kishie	19
Croft at Cunningsburgh	21
North Esplanade, Lerwick – *J. D. Rattar*	24
A Shetland Burn – *J. D. Rattar*	25
Ailsa	26
Gulberwick – *J. D. Rattar*	27
Rachel	28
Georgia – *M. Coleman*	30
Hillswick, Shetland – © *The Shetland Times Ltd.*	31
Anderson E. Institute, Lerwick – *J. D. Rattar*	32
Gloup, Yell – *J. D. Rattar*	34
Leaving Home – *Painting by R. J. Robertson*	36
Commercial Street, Lerwick – *J. D. Rattar*	41
Fair Isle	43
Widows Homes, Lerwick – *J. D. Rattar*	46
Great Black-Backed Gull – *J. D. Rattar*	47
Dunrossness church	48
Sandwick – *J. D. Rattar*	51
Bigton – *J. D. Rattar*	54
Ireland – *J. D. Rattar*	55
The Slipway – *J. D. Rattar*	56

Mousa

The evening was still
The atmosphere warm
As we waited at Sandlodge slip.
The day was ending
The excitement beginning
As we boarded the Mousa ship.

The place we left
Was much the same
As the island that lay off-shore.
But magic was there
And enchanting tales
Of old picts and Viking lore.

If only they knew
The peace we see
In an island empty of men –
The calm peerie selkie
The quiet cute lamb –
Till the place is invaded again.

We wanted only fun
The chance to dream
Of our Thule lovely and fair,
Where people are friends,
God's creatures are safe
And island life is beyond compare.

Young Love - *Norway 900AD*

When I saw you by the shore
your spirit touched me tenderly
and all at once I felt an affinity
that pierced deep in my soul.

And all at once the joy and thrill,
and hurt and torment, mixed themselves
in a confusion of emotion
which brought me blissful pain.

Your kin and mine, I thought,
would never give their blessing.
I went to turn and run, and spare
you grief – but I could not.

I was captured by your charm.
You seemed quiet and shy
but your eyes sparkled
in an enchanting kind of way.

You smiled like the sunlight
shimmering on the water,
so bright and radiant
so warm and welcoming.

You spoke and your voice
was calm and gentle;
and I listened in a trance
that I hoped would never end.

Tomorrow we will be parted.
Go back to your folk and forget me.
Unless you would risk all
for a life of adventure and love.

Erlend and Margaret - *Shetland 1153AD*

Who said we were past it
And that we're far too old:
Love is not just for youth.

Who said we've lost feeling
And that we just can't care:
Passion knows no age.

Who said our hearts are grey
And that our bliss is gone:
Tenderness is always there.

Who said the Tower won't shelter
And that love can't conquer all:
Gently we touch - and love is sealed.

The young couple fled to Shetland, were shipwrecked and found shelter at Mousa Broch.
The older couple pursued by the woman's son, Earl Harald, also found refuge in the Broch.

The Ruin at Westerwick

Who dwelt
in days gone by
within these walls
that now stand naked
to the elements?

What old woman
sat with sock in hand –
and gossip on lips –
by the open fire
and poked the peats
when uninvited draughts
chilled the air?

What old man
sat with pipe in mouth
and revelled in tales
of Greenland whaling
and far-haaf fishing,
of uncan folk and scary seas,
and then spat at the fire
    to clear his throat?

What wife
chained herself
to house and yard –
when he was at the fishing –
and looked after young and old,
and the dispensation of rumours
    – all demanding,
and then attended kye?

What man
visited here twice a week
in summer;
and in winter lost his strength
digging, building, mending,
in a drudgery
whose only escape was the haaf?

What peerie lass
played at the doors
and transformed herself
with a smile
into a princess,
or the perfect mother
with a cribful of bairns?

What peerie boy
ranted round the croft,
and with serious intent
turned crub into castle,
and rigged up a boat,
and dreamt of
war and adventure?

What stories
these stones could tell;
yet keep the secret
of toil and sweat,
and love and tears,
and tales and dreams ...
of days gone by.

Mattie's Trip ta Lerrick

Mattie stopped aff at da restin ston
be da nort end o Cunnisburgh.
Hit wis a lang trek to Lerrick.
You got nae better deal dere
bit dere wir mair shops
an mair o a choice –
an relations ta veesit!

Mattie set doon her kishie,
foo o a fortnight's makkin –
an her best Sunday shön
(naebody wore rivlins i da toon).
She aet her floory bannock
an drank her skaar o milk.
It wisna much, but it was anyoch.

She began ta look aboot her
at da scatterin o croft hooses,
each wan wi a straen röf.
Een or twa wir gettin mended.
Da streen had wept a relentless doontöm –
blankets an furnitir stood i da sun.
Women wir dellin i da yerds.

Mattie toucht fir a meenit.
Wid life ivir git ony better?
Da owld folk used ta tell o days
whan life wis really herd –
maybe wan day she wid be tellin
her grandbairns da sam story;
maybe wan day life wid be aesier.

Nae mair strent-sappin struggle on laand,
nae mair precarious strivin at sea,
nae mair dependin on your sock
fir da twartree essentials you needed;
an nae mair trekkin
back an fore ta Lerrick or Scallowa
wi a kishie apon your back ...

Hit wis time ta whet dreamin.
Dere wis a lang rod ahead,
an a langer een back.
Mattie hoisted her kishie,
set her face ta da nort,
prayed dat her maakin wid sell
an laid an aamos on her bairns.

Journey to Wick

It was an awful pilgrimage to make.
Aunty Mary's lay in ruins that I hardly recognised.
Where was the porch, where the sheds and byre
that ran with hens and chickens?
Where the flags that lay before the door
and where was the door through which
we entered into an even earlier age?

The peerie pokie windows were still there though,
the ones that allowed just enough light
to lift a dismal gloom
and shed a shaft of brightness
into that dark and dreary room.

My memories fade but in my mind I saw
the old black stove,
the dark brown seat, the darker bunks
discreetly set in the background,
the dresser covered in fancy crockery that was never used,
and in the middle of the room hanging from the ceiling
the flycatcher – smelly and covered with insects;
the press at the side filled with uninviting food –
the basics was all she needed or indeed wanted,
the table heaped with her "essentials" of life –
her papers and magazines
and just a little space for teacups, condensed milk,
damp sugar and plain biscuits;

And beyond, the window sill with its ornaments
and odd bits and pieces
and beyond, the window which brought a shaft of light
into that dark and dreary room.

My memories fade but some things cannot be forgotten.
The generations come and go – they say,
but they come and go no more at Wick.
For at Wick they have gone – gone forever,
and with them have gone the hopes and dreams
and schemes of a romantic exile.

The Contentment of the Uneasy Chair

You sit by the fireside
in an uneasy chair
pipe planted firmly
beneath your wide moustache.
And there you mull over
a mixture of mottled memories.

It is neither your chair nor fireside!
Having spent the past year and a half
with your old sister-in-law,
you are now in the equally
uncomfortable company
of your younger sister.

Yet you sit contented
amidst so much discontentment.

You were a young man
when first you were driven
from your own fireside –
and that by your own father!
Though he was just the mouth
for the tantrums of ill-natured
vindictive women,
in turn manipulated
by a clever scheming craetir
who wanted the place for himself.
You found rooms in the town.

And there you sat contented
amidst so much discontentment.

You spent your life
driven from your fireside,
by your need to earn
and by your love of the sea.
Though who could have blamed you
if you had tarried
on a worrying winter's day.
Yet to the uncomfortable accommodation
of your boat you gladly went.
And on a stormy night
were battered by the wind's wild fury.

And there you sat contented
amidst so much discontentment.

Eventually your life's work done
you came ashore for peace and calm,
but found yourself once more
driven from your own fireside.
This time fate had taken a hand
and led you from the hearth
and left you homeless for your comfort.
Your wife's sister offered chair and bed,
and gratefully accepted
your rent in advance.

And there you sat for a time contented
amidst so much discontentment.

How can you sit so contented
amidst so much discontentment?
How can you combat so well
the tantrums of women and weather –
and the treachery of those whose loyalty
you should have expected without question?

You draw on your pipe, and remove it
from beneath your wide moustache.
And with a contented calming smile
you quietly reply,
"It's better to agree, than go to law
and lose your self-respect."

Expectant Joy

I carried you in hope
I watched you grow with glee
I felt you kick and move
So active though so wee.

You inspired in me great love
And many a happy smile
You made me stop and think
And dream of you awhile.

I planned so many things
That we would do together
Of sights that we would see
Of love to last forever.

Where are you now I wonder,
Why did we have to part?
Though now so far away,
You remain yet in my heart.

Ailsa

How helplessly you lay there
Quiet and gentle and sweet
A hap about your shoulders
And flowers beside your feet.

You slept amid the bustling,
Newborn and without a care
You knew that you were safe
Held in a mother's prayer.

The sun came in the window
And caressed your lovely face
Your head lit up with light
Your soul seemed filled with grace.

Your eyes began to open
What lay in store for you
May all you see be good
May all you know be true.

A Baptismal Blessing

I look at the hills
And think of the past
And of those who dwelt here before.
The children who played
by beach and by burn
beneath the sun of a long summer's day.
May this bairn know the same freedom and fun
The same care of a family's love
And may they know every day of their life
The care of their Father above.

A Sunny Day with Rachel

Today has been one of those days
when the sun has shone.
And reflecting the golden sun
has been a host of golden daffodils.

Today has been one of those days
when everything has smiled.
And reflecting the bright gladness
has been a host of happy faces.

Today has been one of those days
when everything has jumped for joy.
And reflecting the exuberance
has been a host of excited bairns.

Today has been one of those days
when warmth has been in the air.
And reflecting the closeness
has been a host of radiant friends.

Georgia

*I met a little girl today
who invited me into her world ...*

You live in a wonderful world of magic ...
of castles and princesses;
and exotic creatures
and cuddly companions
and cute peerie cronies –
bright inanimate toys to us
but to you comrades
in your extra-terrestrial travels.

What adventures lie in store this day ...
A visit to the palace of sunshine,
of undisturbed peace and happiness,
where girls bask in the glory of charm
and polite conversation
and whispers of intrigue.
And which porcelain friend will go with you
for company and to add a touch of class?

Or maybe you are dreaming of
a trip over fields with your peerie pony
prancing on carpets of golden buttercups
 and crimson clover
to the sparkling sea by Ninian's silver sands.
And there to meet in your mind
the mermaids by the shore
or the selkies who live in a world that only you
with your elfin spirit can enter.

And what if your eye should stray to old Foula?
Will your pony take flights of fancy
to Thule's Tir na n-Og?
And with the solan and scarf
glide your way to the land of eternal youth,
where only children exist
in their own dream world
of happy games and friendship.

O what dreams you dream!
And may all your dreams come true.

May you never lose your child-like charm
that looks for the best in every- one and thing.
May the magic of your imagination
become our reality –
so that we can begin to appreciate
the wonder of what you see
in creatures, and countryside, and characters –
in their beauty and in their charm.

A Lovely Peerie Bairn

"Handicapped," they say. "Poor thing!"
And yet you run around
carefree – with energy and strength
and with the curiosity
of any peerie bairn.

There's laughter on your face
and mischief in your eyes
and love in your soul –
and we give you our pity!

Pity help us that are not like you!

There's gloom on our faces
and docile acceptance in our eyes
and torment in our souls –
what handicaps we carry – poor things.

Our only curiosity is to know
what next will befall us –
we who are handicapped.

The School

From within these ancient walls
Come memories of learning
And of those whose wisdom and influence
Have never left us

From within these ancient walls
Come thoughts of those
Who kept the maxim of the founder
"Dö weel and persevere."

From within these ancient walls
Come the idealism and dreams
Of those who sought to make a difference
And persevered till they succeeded.

The Bride

You came with a bundle of hopes and dreams
To the kirk by the sea;
You came nervous and excited
To stand at the altar
To stand by the one you loved.

As you came the rain fell freely
Mingling with your tears of joy and emotion;
As you came the mist gathered in
Encircling like the silk shawl about your shoulders
Encircling like the love and security you had found.

As you came there was no sun to shine
But your eyes sparkled with bright intensity;
As you came the air was chilled and damp
Yet inside you were warm and radiant
And your warmth and radiance glowed.

Having come there were voices to hear
But your emotions said more;
Having come there were vows to repeat
Yet your promises were already fastened in your heart
Your promises to the one you loved.

Having come it was time to go
To celebrate with wine and laughter;
Having come it was time to share a song of gladness
With those who wished you joy and happiness
With loved ones and with the one you loved.

The Wedding – at Cullivoe

Heraldic clouds stood round the hall of heaven
Whose walls were brightly painted blue;
The sun smiled blessing on the earth,
And those in love rejoiced in grateful praise.

An heraldic saint stood in the chancel window
Remembering those who gave their lives for us.
A couple came to kirk for holy blessing,
And kith and kin sang loud in joyful praise.

Heraldic shields stood round the village hall
And spoke of those who came here long ago.
A crowd gathered round for happy celebration,
And with the two joined in the dance of praise.

Ode to Dr Robertson – *Just Perfect*

Hit wisna whit I hed imagined,
Whit in my mind's eye I saa –
Da harbour, da boats and da shops
Or even da impressive Toon Ha'.

Da skyline filled wi beeldins
O aa manner o sizes and forms,
And da calm o da Bressa Sund
Whaar da boats are safe fae da storms.

Bit afore me da Knab and da Ness
Aa happed in a coverin o snow,
And da Boat gaan oot be da Light
Startin tae toss to and fro.

Da Boat's no da Clair dat I minded.
Shö's da new wan aa blue and white.
Bit da backgrund is as owld as can be –
A never changin landscape o delight.

Only da wadder changes da scene,
And of coorse man's interferin haand,
Bit du's decked hit wi a blanket o snow
Tae remind wis hit's really God's laand.

Da hills and rocks are aye wi wis
Even whan wir vaegin awa.
Though da Boat taks wis sooth tae anidder life
We dunna forgit dem ava.

Nedder do we forgit da memories dey hadd
O faemily an folk loved an kent,
O pleasures an wark an shared joy
And da pain o laevin dem ahint.

So du sees, dy idea wis better as mine
Whit du's draain and pented wis sae right
Ta gie tae an exile in a place far awa,
Just perfect ta remind her o a weel loved sight.

The Knitting

*She seeks wool
and works with willing hands ...*

Another day at the fireside
not chosen idleness
but imposed necessity.

Food had to go on the table
and claes on bairns' backs.
But out of necessity
came the creation,
that the better-off
wore with pride.

Still there was no time
for social philosophy.
No time to dream
of what might have been.

She picked up her sock –
a 'special' for Tulloch's –
and checked the loops,
and her cloos of wirsit.

And her well-worn fingers
entwined with wool,
began to dance
to a familiar rhythm
and colour and beauty and warmth
were created.

The Peat Hill

The cry of the curlew
accompanied the flash of steel
in the heather-clad moor.
Reluctantly the fell
parted from the peat
and with a dull thud
landed in the greff.

The tushkar slid into the bank
and the first fuel was flung out.
The dyke grew in stages
with a thousand windows
seeking wind.

In days, the dyke
turned into huddles
of tall standing stooks
inviting sun and breeze
and shading hardening clods.

The scene surveyed
confirmed that there would be
warmth in the winter hearth.
A satisfied smile spread on the lips
in prospect of heat in the bones.

And the curlew cried farewell
for another year.

Lerwick after the Last Half-Century

How different the old town looks
dragged into modern times
with a mixture of add-ons
to what were once neat houses,
and new buildings
of dull demoralising concrete.
The old and the new merging
in an uncomfortable contradiction.
Gardens which once stood proud
now sit in a sorry state of shame.
Though here and there
some inspirational well-kept
splashes of colour
lift the spirits.

The shoreline meanders by the same route
and rocks stand firm
in the changeful moods of the sea.
But where are the children
that on a bright blue day
once gathered to enjoy the exhilaration
of a dip at the Waari Geo?
Selkies have taken their place
and frolic as once we did
in the icy waters
of that peaceful bay.

Entering the street from the South End
brought back memories
of music at the High Jinks
and ice cream at Solotti's –
though it's hard to remember
what was sold in premises
that today are devoted to charities.

Peter Leisk's my favourite haunt
now dispenses information,
where in childhood days
we had the agonising choice,
in that mecca of confectionery,
of how to spend threepence.

And how we relished
the pleasure of eating out.
A patty supper at the pier-head –
carefully packaged by peerie Johan!
The Steamer Store is but a memory
and crowds that bid the Boat farewell
and exchanged friendly conversation
no longer have cause to gather.

The girls, our companions today,
(I wonder what they will see
in another half-century)
are getting tired and hungry,
but know their favourite haunts
which, for a pound or two,
will hand over the soul-restoring delights
of whipped ice cream – in three flavours –
or chips presented in a polystyrene cup.
What I wonder now happens to the newspapers
that used to gather our Saturday feast?

The girls blow on their chips
and later cover their chins
in milky white;
and their quiet contentment
tells us that some things
will never change!

Pictures on the Wall – for JDR

I first met you
on our living room wall.
Your black framed windows
opening a view to a bygone age
that fascinated my childhood imagination.

I wanted to reach back
and touch that world
uncluttered with modern worries
of wealth, and the technology
that easing the bones
attacks the spirit
strangling our progress
to a rich rewarding life.

There was a time when you appeared
with so many scenes, in so many places –
a junk shop in Wales, a forgotten attic,
a Harry Hay sale – your favourite haunt,
a bedroom in Fife – where you belonged
to an old man who could not forget
his first love from Scalloway!
Each time the thrill of discovering
your ancient impressions
brought me a special joy
and opened yet another view
to a time I longed to touch.

But what was life really like
in that idyllic age?
In their poverty people had a rich love
of land and sea and sky.
And in the struggle of living
found time for each other.

The Storm

With wild intent you gathered strength,
And battered holms and crashed on cliffs;
And in spiteful mood you sent salt spray
To drench both land and beast.

What occasioned your uncontrolled fury
That with an awesome haunting howl
Swept menacingly from the west
To cause confusion to land and beast.

All night you made your grievance known
And fearful of your force we cowered inside,
Yet in the morning you still refused
To surrender land and beast.

The day has worn far – and you are gone
To grip and grieve some other place;
And here the sun now shines –
Restoring peace, to land and beast.

(Fair Isle : Friday 26th April, 2002)

Grant

The raging storm reflected our feelings
The day we laid our child to rest.
The wind battered our bodies
As the tragedy had battered our emotions.
The rain mingled with our tears
Together they ran down our cheeks.
The cold chilled us to the core
And we felt numbed outside and in.

From the shore we saw the sea in turmoil
It tried to match the turmoil in our hearts
The waves battered the rocks
As we had been battered these past days.
The darkness of the clouds
Darkened our spirits still further.
It was such a bleak day
And such a bleak occasion.

Yet from somewhere we gathered the strength
To cope with the wild unsettling storm.
The crowd began to enclose us
And in our grief we saw that many cared.
We felt the comfort of their shelter
And we knew that we were not alone.
Surely God cared too
And his comfort would shelter us in days to come.

Then we thought of Grant ...
His ready smile, his willing friendly spirit ...
Somehow happy memories shone through
Despite this day of dismal grief.
We could not forget him
Nor would we ... he would always have
A special place in our hearts,
And we would remember him with joy and love.

Bryan

One day the sun is shining brightly
And our world is just perfect;
The next day grey rain pours down
On the bleakness of our existence.

Last night we sang Viking songs
Of celebration and boldness;
Today we sing simple psalms
In a sadness seeking consolation.

Yes we do believe in yesterday
When with confident courage
We could have faced and tackled
Any kind of torment or trouble.

We had your bright smiling face
We had your assured presence;
Together nothing could beat us,
We'd face the world in any mood.

But you are gone, gone for ever;
You have left too many broken hearts
Too many shattered dreams.
Too many confused emotions.

But you have also left a precious legacy,
A priceless treasure to sustain our souls;
The memory of your love and care
Will brighten up bleak days of sorrow.

The happiness and hopes we shared
Will never fade and never be forgotten;
Your bright, cheery, confident spirit
Will lead us in our uncertain future.

The Widow's Mites

He's gone – left a widow wi bairns.
Whit'll come o dem.

"Keep a shillin i dee purse,
and a packet o Brooke Bond i da press,"
counselled a friend.
"Du'll be able ta set doon a cup o tae,
if ony een comes."

Bit whit use is keepin face fir hungry bairns.
Dir stamachs dunna care whit ony een says.
Whan it's time ta aet, fine wirds 'll no fill dem up.
No even good wishes, or sympathetic smiles
dat tink dae understaand.

"Mam is it tattie soup again taday?"
– A scowl o hurt and horror ...
"Mam I lik tattie soup."

Candice

I did not go with quiet resignation
I did not slip away from life not caring
I did not leave knowing your hearts would hurt
Knowing I would give a legacy of grief and pain.

I did not live with quiet resignation
You filled me with too much life for that
You gave me a spirit of adventure
Of daring to believe that I could conquer all.

I did not care with quiet resignation
Each of you was a precious love to me
There was room in my heart for all
But for my peerie boy, a very special place.

Do not leave here with quiet resignation
Do not slip away with grief and pain
But go out with bold joy, and bright courage
And my memory and my spirit will live on.

Great Black-Backed Gull
Photo J.D.Rattar

Memories Shared are Given Forever

Thou the miles hae scattered wis
We're no sae far apairt
Da towts we hae and da memories dear
Are closs tae mind and hert.

Du geed fae wis a while ago
Ta live apo da 'Rock'
We mind da days dat we wir dere
And pictir dee among da folk.

Hoo we wissed we could've shared
Mair o dy life and talk
Hit wid a med da rod ahead
A peerie bit aesier tae walk.

Though du's gone tae dy eternal rest
We're no jüst gaan ta pairt
We'll mind da days o lang ago
And treasure dee in wir hert.

At The Ness Kirk

The rain summed up our bitter grief
Falling freely as our tears
How can so much go so wrong
And leave us with new fears.

Sister and father so soon together.
And memories long since gone
Come back to life, as we remember
When mother left us all alone.

How cruel life, it takes so much
So much we can't get back
Only our memories console our thoughts
And them it cannot take.

We look up from our troubled tears
To see the sombre clad
So many stand to share our grief
And begin to make us glad.

We are not on our own today
The countless tarry awhile
With comfort, an embrace, a kiss
They make us share a smile.

With weary steps we leave this place.
Thank God for those who share
Grief for those we loved so much
And leave now to God's care.

Kathleen

Du wid lie dere
An dy eyes wid look oot apon wis.
Sometimes dey spaak ta wis
An sometimes dey wir joost too tired.
Bit usually whan some een cam ta see dee
Dy eyes wid brighten up wi interest.
Dir wis a sparkle dere
Lik da sun apon da waater.
Whit stories du wanted ta tell
O days lang ago
Da laughter an joys o youth
Da bright days o happy pleasure.

Whan some een cam ta care
Dy eyes shaad foo grateful du wis.
Du wis in dir haands
Hoo du wished it could have been idder.
Du fowt so weel, du nivir gied up
Du wis determined ta keep da upper haand.
Yet dere du wis lyin helpless in bed ...

But lyin dere du hed sae much ta gie ta idders.
Du shaad wis patience an courage
Strent in waekness, laughter in pain,
An da determination ta haad in dere
An nivir lit it git dee doon.
Du pat courage in wis
An du med wis humble.

Whan some een cam ta pray wi dee
Dy eyes wid fill up wi tears –
hit wis da only wye dy emotion could win oot.
Whit pain du must hae siffered.
But du looked ta Him fir comfort
An for sense, whaar we could see non
An fir release fae da prison dat du wis in.
Du haes dat release noo ...
An joost as du's hed a share o His sifferin
Du'll certainly hae a share o His glory.

Gathered Grief

It was a day full of fun and joy
A day with family and friends
And bairns rantin' round
A day when we laughed and sighed
The day that our Dad died.
How could happiness turn so sad
And sunshine and peace and perfect bliss
Turn to turmoil, and abject grief and dark despair.

That night as our tears fell freely
The heavens joined in and wept with floods of rain.
As morning broke everything was still in tears
And dark brown burns with gathered grief
Cascaded their gloomy emotions down the hills.
But even the burns in spate
Could not match the overwhelming grief we felt
In the days when our Dad died.

At night the darkness and gloom
Merged with our mood
In a harmony of black despair.
The stars shone dimly – too far away
To offer any comfort.
The moon hid itself behind the clouds
And nothing dared disturb our dreadful grief
In the days when our Dad died.

But then we saw a face
A familiar face of fun and laughter
A face that cheered up many a day of darkness.
"Weep no more for me" he said.
"My body's gone but not my heart and soul.
I'll hold you always in my care
Until the day when we will share
A fuller love with God up here
In the bliss of heavenly peace."

A Quiet and Gentle Life

You went from us
as you had lived with us
so quietly and gently.
You left a deep void in our lives,
and a deep impression in our hearts.

We will miss your smile,
your ready encouragement.
And we will miss your caring,
for "the teaching of kindness,
was always on your tongue."

We will remember your knitting –
how your fingers danced
to familiar rhythms
to produce exquisite beauty.
In your heart you wove patterns
of an even greater beauty
through your kind and loving care.

We will remember your music –
how your fingers danced
to familiar rhythms
to produce exquisite tunes.
The music of your heart
struck a cord in our souls
and inspired in us joy and peace.

May the pattern of your kind and loving care
and the music that inspired joy and peace
always dance familiar rhythms
in our hearts and lives.
And we will smile your ready encouragement
and the teaching of your kindness,
will always be on our tongues.

Maggie Ann

Bigton stood in perfect peace
The day we laid a saint to rest
Her struggling and her striving done
Her well-earned rest was finally won.

The sun caressed old Ninian's isle
Which pointed far out to the west
Where Foula rose in majesty ~
And God whispered, come to me.

Maggie Ann we honour you
You gave so much to those so near
You lived with courage and with love
God will reward you up above.

Those we have loved

A crowded kirk in gathered grief
Bid farewell to a special soul.
Her suffering done, they came to hear,
Of her life and love, her joys and woe.

Her resting place on Ireland's shore
Across the water from Ninian's isle,
A fitting site for a gentle saint
Who gave her life for those she loved.

Four figures lingered by a stone
And shared a solemn moment there.
Tears and hugs and a memory sore
Bound them closely in a common gloom.

Lord on that day our world looked fair
With sparkling sea and sun-soaked land.
But surely there's yet a better place
For those we've loved and lost awhile.

IRELAND, SHETLAND   PHOTO J. D. RATTAR

A'm stravaged ta places roond da eart
An seen some windrous sights
Bit nithin compares ta da Northern Isles
An its endless simmer nights.
I wander doon aboot da Docks
An mind da days o' youth
Da days dat wir sae bright.